ANI DIFRANCO

VERSES

RIGHTEOUS BABE
Buffalo, New York

7 SEVEN STORIES PRESS
New York · London · Melbourne · Toronto

SEVEN STORIES PRESS
140 Watts Street, New York, NY 10013
www.sevenstories.com

In Canada
Publishers Group Canada,
559 College Street,
Toronto, ON M6G 1A9

In the UK
Turnaround Publisher Services Ltd.,
Unit 3, Olympia Trading Estate, Coburg Road,
Wood Green, London N22 6TZ

In Australia
Palgrave Macmillan,
15-19 Claremont Street,
South Yarra, VIC 3141

RIGHTEOUS BABE
341 Delaware Avenue, Buffalo, NY 14202
www.righteousbabe.com

LIBRARY OF CONGRESS CATALOGING-IN-PUBLICATION DATA
DiFranco, Ani.
Ani DiFranco : verses / by Ani DiFranco.—1st ed.
p. cm.
ISBN 978-1-58322-823-4 (paper over board)
I. Title.
PS3604.I385A55 2007
811'.6—dc22
2007025604

College professors may order examination copies of Seven Stories Press titles for a free six-month trial period. To order, visit www.sevenstories.com/textbook or fax on school letterhead to (212) 226-1411.

Design by Ani DiFranco, Brian Grunert, and Kyle Morrissey
Printed in the United States of America.
9 8 7 6 5 4 3 2 1

for Sekou

PART I

COMING UP

PART II
SELF EVIDENT

PART I
COMING UP

COMING UP

our father who art in a penthouse
sits in his 37th floor suite
and swivels
to gaze down at the city he made me in
he allows me to stand
and solicit graffiti
until he needs the land i stand on

and i in my darkened threshold
am pawing through my pockets
the receipts
the bus schedules
the matchbook phone numbers
urgent napkin poems
all of which laundering has rendered
pulpy and strange
loose change
and a key
ask me
go ahead

ask me if i care—
i got the answer here
i wrote it down somewhere
i just gotta find it

and somebody and their spray paint
got too close
somebody came on too heavy
now look at me
made ugly by the drooling letters
i was better off alone
ain't that the way it is?
they don't know the first thing
but you don't know that
'til they take the first swing
my fingers are red and swollen from the cold
i'm getting bold in my old age
so go ahead

try the door

it doesn't matter any more
i know the weak hearted are strong willed
and we're being kept alive until we're killed

he's up there
the ice is clinking in his glass
he sends us little pieces of paper
i don't ask
i just empty my pockets
and wait
it's not fate
it's just circumstance
i don't fool myself with romance
i just live phone number to phone number
dusting them against my thighs in the warmth of my pockets
which whisper history incessantly asking me
where were you?

i lower my eyes
wishing i could cry more
and care less
yes it's true
i was trying to love someone again
i was caught caring
bearing weight
but i love this city
this state
this country
is too large
and whoever's in charge up there
had better take the elevator down and put more than
change in our cup
or else we
are coming
up

MY IQ

when i was 4 years old
they tried to test my iq
they showed me this picture
of three oranges and a pear
they asked me
which one is different and does not belong?
they taught me different
is wrong

but when i was 13 years old
i woke up one morning
thighs covered in blood
like a war
like a warning
that i live in a breakable takeable body
an ever-increasingly valuable body
that a woman had come in the night to replace me
deface me

see my body is borrowed
i got it on loan
for the time in between my mom and some maggots
i don't need anyone to hold me
i can hold my own
i got highways for stretch marks
see where i've grown?

and i sing sometimes
like my life is at stake
cuz you're only as loud
as the noises you make
i'm learning to laugh
as hard as i can listen
cuz silence is violence
in women and poor people
if more people were screaming then i could relax
but a good brain ain't diddly if you don't have the facts

we live in a breakable takeable world
an ever available possible world
and we can make music
like we can make do
genius is in a backbeat
backseat to nothing if you're dancing
especially something stupid
like iq
for every lie i unlearn
i learn something new
and i sing sometimes
for the war that i fight
cuz every tool is a weapon
if you hold it right

LITERAL

when they said he could walk on water
what it sounds like to me

is he could float like a butterfly
and sting like a bee

literal people are scary, man
literal people scare me

out there trying to rid the world of its poetry

while getting it wrong fundamentally
down at the church of "look!
it says right here, see!"

THE SLANT

the slant
a building settling
around me my
figure female
framed crookedly
in the threshold
of the room
door scraping floor boards
with every opening
carving a rough history
of bedroom scenes
the plot
hard to follow
the text
obscured
in the folds of sheets slowly
gathering the stains of seasons
spent lying there
red and brown
like leaves fallen
the colors of an eternal cycle
fading with the wash cycle
and the rinse cycle
again an un-
familiar smell
like my name misspelled
or misspoken
a cycle broken

the sound of them strong stalking
talking about their prey
like the way
hammer meets nail
pounding
they say
pounding out the rhythms
of attraction
like a woman
was a drum
like a body
was a weapon
like there was something more they wanted
than the journey
like it was owed to them
steel-toed they walk
and i'm wondering why
this fear of men?
maybe it's cuz i'm hungry
and like a baby
i'm dependent on them
to feed me
i am a work in progress
dressed in the fabric of a world unfolding
offering me intricate patterns of questions
rhythms that never come clean
and strengths
that you still haven't seen

32 FLAVORS

squint your eyes and look closer
i'm not between you and your ambition
i am a poster girl with no poster
i am thirty-two flavors and then some
and i'm beyond your peripheral vision
so you might wanna turn your head
cuz some day you are going to get hungry
and eat most of the words you just said

both my parents taught me about goodwill
and i have done well by their names
just the kindness i've lavished on strangers
is more than i can explain
still there's many who've turned out their porch lights
just so i would think they were not home
and hid in the dark of their windows
'til i passed and left them alone

and god help you if you are an ugly girl
course too pretty is also your doom
cuz everyone harbors a secret hatred
for the prettiest girl in the room
god help you if you are a phoenix
and you dare to rise up from the ash
a thousand eyes will smolder with jealousy
while you are just flying past

i never tried to give my life meaning
by demeaning you
and i would like to state for the record
i did everything that i could do
i'm not saying that i am a saint
i just don't wanna live that way
no i will never be a saint
but i will always say

squint your eyes and look closer
i'm not between you and your ambition
i am a poster girl with no poster
i am thirty-two flavors and then some
and i'm beyond your peripheral vision
so you might wanna turn your head
cuz some day you might find you are starving
and eating all of the words that you said

ANGEL FOOD

if the mattress was a tabletop
and the bedsheet was a page
we'd be written out
like a couple of question marks
my convex to your concave
and we'd be lying here
at the end of a sentence
that asks, are you ready now?
are you gonna glow in the dark?
are you gonna show me how?

do you like to watch when water misbehaves?
do you like waves?
as the wind shifts
and shifts again
the sail smiles
and gently slaps around the mast
ballast
ballast
ballast

when you come to me
come to me with cake
in your pocket
come to me nicely
with that soft kinda cake
that's mostly icing
come to me ready and rude
bring me angel food
angel food

FUEL

they were digging a new foundation in manhattan
and they discovered a slave cemetery there
may their souls rest easy
now that lynching is frowned upon
and we've moved on
to the electric chair
and i wonder who's gonna be president
tweedle dumb or tweedle dumber?
and who's gonna have the big blockbuster box office
this summer?
maybe we should put up a wall
between the houses and the highway
and then you can go your way
and i can go my way

except all the radios agree with all the tv's
and the magazines agree with all the radios
and i keep hearing that same damn song
everywhere i go
everywhere i go
maybe i should put a bucket over my head
and a marshmallow in each ear
and stumble around for another dumb numb week
for another hum drum hit song to appear
people used to make records
as in a record of an event
the event of people
playing music in a room
now everything is cross-marketing
it's about sunglasses and shoes
or guns and booty
you choose

we got it rehashed
we got it half-assed
we're digging up all the graves
and we're spitting on the past
and we can choose between the colors
of the lipstick on the whores
cuz we know the difference
between the font of twenty percent more
and the font of teriyaki
you tell me—
how does it make you feel?
you tell me—
what's real?

they say that alcoholics are always alcoholics
even when they're as dry as my lips for years
even when they're stranded on a small desert island
with no place in two thousand miles to buy beer
and i wonder
is he different?
is he different?
has he changed?
what he's about
or is he just a liar
with nothing to lie about?
am i headed for the same brick wall?
is there anything i can do
about anything at all?

except go back to that corner in manhattan
and dig deeper
dig deeper this time
down beneath the impossible pain of our history
beneath unknown bones
beneath the bedrock of the mystery
beneath the sewage system and the path train
beneath the cobblestones and the water main
beneath the traffic of friendships and street deals
beneath the screeching of kamikaze cab wheels
beneath everything i can think of to think about
beneath it all
beneath all get out
beneath the good and the kind and the stupid and the cruel
there's a fire that's just waiting for fuel

KNOW NOW THEN

it's not so much that we got closer
it's that her face just got bigger
and by the time it was filling up my whole view
i figured my face had got bigger too
so i used it to try and sway her
say something to her
make my case
but my face
never had a chance
all along it was the wrong song and dance
i just stood there
without even a stance
helpless to her advance
and her retreat
backspace, delete

it wasn't so much that we fell in love as
my life just seemed to come down
to a slow walk on a straight line
between her smile and her frown
and maybe we never were as close
as we should have been
but i didn't know
what i know now then
yeah i didn't know what i
know now then

PULSE

you crawled into my bed that night
like some sort of giant insect
and i found myself spellbound
at the sight of you
beautiful and grotesque
and all the rest of that bug stuff
bluffing your way into my mouth
behind my teeth
reaching for my scars
that night we got kicked out of two bars
and laughed our way home

that night you leaned over
and threw up into your hair
and i held you there, thinking
i would offer you my pulse
if i thought it would be useful
i would give you my breath
except the problem with death
is we have somehundred years
and then they can build buildings
on our only bones
a hundred years and then your grave is not your own

and we lie in our beds and our graves
unable to save ourselves
from the quaint tragedies we invent and undo
from the stupid circumstances we slalom through
and i realized that night
that the hall light
which seemed so bright when you turned it on
is nothing
compared to the dawn
which is nothing
compared to the light which seeps from me while you're sleeping
cocooned in my room
beautiful and grotesque
resting
that night we got kicked out of two bars
and laughed our way home
i thought:
i would offer you my pulse
i would give you my breath
i would offer you my pulse...

AS IS

you can't hide
behind social graces
so don't try
to be all touchy feely
cuz you lie
in my face of all places
but i got no
problem with that really

what bugs me
is that you believe what you're saying
what bothers me
is that you don't know how you feel
what scares me
is that while you're telling me stories
you actually
believe that they are real

i got no illusions about you
guess what?
i never did
when i say
when i say i'll take it
i mean
i always mean as is

just give up
and admit you're an asshole
you would be
in some good company
and i think you'd find
that your friends would forgive you
or maybe i
am just speaking for me

cuz when i look around
i think this
this is good enough
and i try to laugh
at whatever life brings
cuz when i look down
i just miss all the good stuff
and when i look up
i just trip over things

i've got no illusions about you
guess what?
i never did
when i say
when i say i'll take it
i mean
i always mean as is

NOT SO SOFT

in a forest of stone
underneath the corporate canopy
where the sun
rarely
filters
down
the ground is not so soft
not so soft

they build buildings
to house people making money
or they build buildings
to make money off housing people
it's true like a lot of things are true

foraging for a phone booth
on the forest floor
that is not so soft
i look up
it looks like the buildings are burning
but it's just the sun setting in the windows
the solar system calling an end to another business day
eternally circling
signaling the rhythmic clicking on and off of computers
the pulse
of the american machine
the pulse
that draws death dancing
out of anonymous side streets
(the ones that always get dumped on
and never get plowed)
it draws dancing
out of little countries
with funny languages
where the ground is getting harder
and it was not that soft
before

those who call the shots
are never in the line of fire
why?
when there is life for hire out there
if a flag of truth were raised
we could watch every liar
rise to wave it

here we learn america
like a script
playwright
birthright
same thing
we bring ourselves to the role
we're all rehearsing for the presidency
i always wanted to be commander in chief
of my one
woman
army

but i can envision the mediocrity
of my finest hour
it's the failed america in me
it is the fear that lives in a forest of stone
underneath the corporate canopy
where the sun
rarely
filters
down
and the ground
is not so soft

THE TRUE STORY OF WHAT WAS

the light blue flickering rhythm
of the neighbor's big console tv
is basking on the ceiling
of another insomniac spree
and outside sleep's open window
between the drops of rain
history is writing a recipe book
for every earthly pain

oh to clean up the clutter of echoes
coming in and out of focus
words spoken like locusts
sing and sing in my head
and thing is
they often seem
in my memory's long dream
to be superfluous to
the true story of what was
cuz
real is real regardless
of what you try to say or say away
real is real relentless
while words distract and dismay
words that change their tune
though the story remains the same
words that fill me quickly
and then are slow to drain
dialogues that dither down reminiscent
of the way it likes to rain
every screen a smoke screen
oh to dream just for a moment
the picture outside the frame

then in a flash
the light blue horizon
spanning a sudden black
is sucked into the vanishing point
and quiet rushes back
to search for the downbeat
in a tabla symphony
to search in the darkness
for someone who looks like me

(though i'm not really who i said i was
or who i thought i'd be)

just a collection of recollections
conversations consisting of the kind of marks we make
when we're trying to get a pen to work again

a lifetime of them!

cough…cough…ahem…

i say to me
now here listening
i say to the locusts
that sing and sing to me sitting
now here on the front porch swing of my eyes:
i hereby amend
whatever i've ever said
with this sigh

32

CLIP CLOP CLACK

a girl with the sun of her youth at her back
and the shadow of her womanhood
before her on the stones
is approaching with a delicate
clip clop clack
her sandals full of toes
that i suppose are headed home

it's early in the evening
and up and down the river
people begin to gather
pearls of laughter
on a strand

i thought solitude would save me
it was pious
it was grand

but the monk that walked beside me
just let go of my hand

TIPTOE

tiptoeing thru the used condoms
strewn on the piers
off the west side highway
sunset behind
the skyline of jersey
walking towards the water
with a fetus holding court in my gut
my body hijacked
my tits swollen and sore
the river has more colors at sunset
than my sock drawer ever dreamed of
i could wake up screaming sometimes
but i don't

i could step off the end of this pier but i got
shit to do and an appointment on tuesday
to shed uninvited blood and tissue
i'll miss you, i say
to the river to the water
to the son or daughter
i thought better of

i could fall in love with jersey
at sunset
but i leave the view to the rats
and tiptoe back

36

SUBDIVISION

white people are so scared of black people
they bulldoze out to the country
and put up houses on little loop-dee-loop streets
and while america gets its heart cut right out of its chest
the berlin wall still runs down main street
separating east side from west
and nothing is stirring, not even a mouse
in the boarded-up stores and the broken-down houses
so they hang colorful banners off all the street lamps
just to prove they got no manners
no mercy and no sense

and i'm wondering what it will take
for my city to rise
first we admit our mistakes
then we open our eyes
the ghosts of old buildings are haunting parking lots
in the city of good neighbors that history forgot

i remember the first time i saw someone
lying on the cold street
i thought: i can't just walk past here
this can't just be true
but i learned by example
to just keep moving my feet
it's amazing the things that we all learn to do

so we're led by denial like lambs to the slaughter
serving empires of style and carbonated sugar water
and the old farm road's a four-lane that leads to the mall
and our dreams are all guillotines waiting to fall

i'm wondering what it will take
for my country to rise
first we admit our mistakes
and then we open our eyes
or nature succumbs to one last dumb decision
and america the beautiful
is just one big subdivision

TAMBURITZA LINGUA

a cold and porcelain lonely
in an old new york hotel
a stranger to a city
that she used to know so well
bathing in a bathroom
that is bathed in the first blue light
of the beginning of a century
at the end of an endless night

then she is wet behind the ears and wafting down the avenue
pre-rush hour
post-rain shower
stillness seeping upward like steam
from another molten sewer
they've been spraying us with chemicals in our sleep
us / they
something about the mosquitoes having some kind of disease
them / me
CIA foul play
if you ask the guy selling hair dryers out of a gym bag
"chemical warfare"
"i'm telling you, lab rat to lab rat!" he says, "that's where the truth is at!"
and everything seems to have gone terribly wrong that can
but one breath at a time is an acceptable plan, she tells herself
and the air is still there
and this morning it's even breathable
and for a second the relief is unbelievable
she's a heavy sack of flour sifted
her burden lifted
she's full of clean wind for one lean moment and then
she's trapped again
reverted
caged and contorted
with no way to get free
(and she's getting plenty of little kisses
but nobody's slippin' her the key)

her whole life a long list of what-ifs
so she doesn't even know where to begin
and the pageantry of suffering therein
rivals television
tv is, after all, the modern day roman coliseum
human devastation as mass entertainment
and now millions sit jeering
collectively cheering
the bloodthirsty hierarchy of the patriarchal arrangement

she is hailing a cab
she is sailing down the avenue
she's 19 going on 30
or maybe she's really 30 now...
it's hard to say
it's hard to keep up with time once it's on its way

besides she never had much of a chance
born into a family built like an avalanche
and somewhere in the 80s between the oat bran and the ozone
she started to figure on things like
why?

one eye pointed upwards looking for the holes in the sky
one eye on the little flashing red light
a picasso face twisted and listing
down the canvas
of the end of an endless night

ten nine eight seven six fivefour
three   two   one
and kerplooey!
you're done.
you're done for.
you're done for good.
so tell me
did you?
did you do?
did you do all you could?

YOUR NEXT BOLD MOVE

coming of age during the plague
of reagan and bush
watching capitalism gun down democracy
it had this funny effect on me
i guess
i am cancer
i am HIV
and i'm down at the blue jesus blue cross hospital
just lookin' up from my pillow
feeling blessed

and the mighty multinationals
have monopolized the oxygen
so it's as easy as breathing
for us all to participate
they're buying and selling off shares of air
and you know it's all around you
but it's hard to point and say there
so you just sit on your hands and quietly contemplate

your next bold move
the next thing you're gonna need to prove
to yourself

what a waste of thumbs that are opposable
to make machines that are disposable
and sell them to seagulls flying in circles around one big right wing
the left wing was broken long ago
by the slingshot of cointelpro
and now it's so hard to have faith
in anything

especially your next bold move
or the next thing you're gonna need to prove
to yourself

you want to track each trickle back to its source
and then scream up the faucet 'til your face is hoarse
cuz you're surrounded by a world's worth of things
you just can't excuse
but you've got the hard cough of a chain smoker
and you're at the arctic circle playing strip poker
and it's getting colder and colder
every time you lose

so go ahead
make your next bold move
tell us
what's the next thing you're gonna need to prove
to yourself?

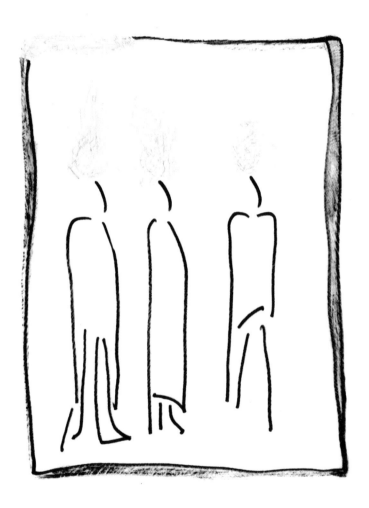

PART II
SELF EVIDENT

SELF EVIDENT

yes
us people are just poems
we're 90% metaphor
with a leanness of meaning
approaching hyper-distillation
and once upon a time
we were moonshine
rushing down the throat of a giraffe
rushing down the long hall
despite what the pa announcement says
rushing down the long stairs
in a building so tall
that it will always be there
yes it's part of a pair
there on the bow of noah's ark
the most prestigious couple
just kickin' back parked
against a perfectly blue sky
on a morning beatific
in its indian summer breeze
on the day that america fell to its knees
after strutting around for a century
without saying thank you
or please
and the shock was subsonic
and the smoke was deafening
between the setup and the punch line
cuz we were all on time for work that day
we all boarded that plane for to fly
and then while the fires were raging
we all climbed up on the windowsill
and then we all held hands
and jumped into the sky
and every borough looked up
when it heard the first blast
and then every dumb action movie
was summarily surpassed
and the exodus uptown by foot and motorcar
looked more like war
than anything i've seen so far

so far

so fierce and ingenious
a poetic specter so far gone
that every jackass newscaster was struck dumb and stumbling
over "oh my god" and "this is unbelievable" and on and on
and i'll tell you what
while we're at it—
you can keep the pentagon
keep the propaganda
keep each and every tv
that's been trying to convince me
to participate in some prep school punk's plan
to perpetuate retribution
perpetuate retribution
even as the blue toxic smoke
of our lesson in retribution
is still hanging in the air
and there's ash on our shoes
and there's ash in our hair
and there's a fine silt on every mantle
from hell's kitchen to brooklyn
and the streets are full of stories
sudden twists and near misses
and soon every open bar is crammed to the rafters
with tales of narrowly averted disasters
and the whiskey is flowin' like never before
as all over the country
folks just shake their heads
and pour

so here's a toast to all the folks who live in palestine
afghanistan
iraq
el salvador
here's a toast to the folks living on the pine ridge reservation
under the stone cold gaze of mount rushmore
here's a toast to all those nurses and doctors
who daily provide women with a choice
who stand down a threat the size of oklahoma city
just to listen to a young woman's voice
and here's a toast to all the folks on death row right now
awaiting the executioner's guillotine
who are shackled there with dread
and can only escape into their heads
to find peace
in the form
of a dream

cuz take away our playstations
and we are a third world nation
under the thumb of some blue blood royal son
who stole the oval office and that phony election
i mean it don't take a weatherman
to look around and see the weather
jeb said he'd deliver florida, folks
and boy did he ever!
and we hold these truths to be self evident:

#1 george w. bush is not president
#2 america is not a true democracy
#3 the media is not fooling me

cuz i am a poem heeding hyper-distillation
i've got no room for a lie so verbose
i'm looking out over my whole human family
and i'm raising my glass in a toast

here's to our last drink of fossil fuels
let us vow to get off of this sauce
shoo away the swarms of commuter planes
and find that train ticket we lost
cuz once upon a time the line followed the river
and peeked into all the backyards
and the laundry was waving
the graffiti was teasing us
from brick walls and bridges
we were rolling over ridges
through valleys
under stars
i dream of touring like duke ellington
in my own railroad car
i dream of waiting on the tall blonde wooden benches
in a grand station aglow with grace
and then standing out on the platform
and feeling the air on my face

give back the night its distant whistle
give the darkness back its soul
give the big oil companies the finger finally
and relearn how to rock-n-roll
yes the lessons are all around us
and a change is waiting there
so it's time to pick through the rubble
clean the streets
and clear the air
get our government to pull its big dick out of the sand
of someone else's desert
put it back in its pants
quit the hypocritical chants of
freedom forever!

cuz when one lone phone rang
in two thousand and one
at ten after nine
on nine one one
which is the number we all called
when that lone phone rang right off the wall
right off our desk and down the long hall
down the long stairs
in a building so tall
that the whole world turned
just to watch it fall

and while we're at it—
remember the first time around?
the bomb?
the ryder truck?
the parking garage?
the princess that didn't even feel the pea?
remember joking around in our apartment on avenue d?

"can you imagine how many paper coffee cups
would have to change their design
following a fantastical reversal of the new york skyline?!"

it was a joke of course
it was a joke
at the time

and that was just a few years ago
so let the record show
that the FBI was all over that case
that the plot was obvious and in everybody's face
and scoping that scene
religiously
the CIA
(or is it KGB?)

committing countless crimes against humanity
with this kind of eventuality
as its excuse
for abuse after expensive abuse
and they didn't have a clue
look
another window to see through
way up here
on the 104th floor
look
another key
another door
10% literal
90% metaphor
3000 some poems disguised as people
on an almost too
perfect
day
should be more than pawns
in some asshole's passion play
so now it's your job
and it's my job
to make it that way
to make sure they didn't die in vain
sshhhhh....
baby listen
hear the train?

IMAGINE THAT

imagine that i am onstage
under a watchtower of punishing light
and in the haze is your face bathed in shadow
and what's beyond you is hidden from sight
and somebody right now is yawning
and watching me like a tv
and i've been frantically piling up sandbags
against the flood waters of fatigue and insecurity

then suddenly i hear my guitar singing
so i just start singing along
and somewhere in my chest all the noise
just gets crushed by the song

imagine that i'm at your mercy
imagine that you are at mine
pretend i've been standing here watching you
watching me all this time
now imagine that you are the weather
in the tiny snow globe of this song
and i am the statue of liberty
one inch long

so here i am at my most hungry
here i am at my most full
here i am waving a red cape
locking eyes with a bull

just imagine that i am onstage
under a watchtower of punishing light
and in the haze is your face bathed in shadow
and what's beyond you is hidden from sight

CALLOUS

you cried and you cried and you cried wolf
so it took me a minute to understand
that you really were hurt bad
that day you deeply cut your hand
and then that look that you gave me
sent me rushing through guilt's door
i'd already started to feel callous
like i really should care more

and it was my work that kept me upright
so you called it a crutch
while i drifted off
into dreams of such and such
and by the time we'd come full circle
we knew exactly what to do
just keep looking at the triangle
instead of what it's pointing to

but you can't will yourself happy
you can't will your cunt wet
you can't keep standing at the station
pretending you're being met
you can't wear a sign that says "yours"
when that ain't what you get

it flows and flows away from me
yes my love is a stream
and your love is a vaudeville show
so charming and obscene
and we both had our moments
we both had our fun
and i hated to prove 'em all right
those who said i'd run

I

earth moving down into night
like it too was his slow whisper

2

swallow my tongue
thick into wishing
and give at my kiss
what pleasure you please

3

make like some anonymous need
came on down there too fast again
and be it love or just this dance
only yes would satisfy

4

oh, great stroke of bare emotional night and unbelievable suck!
i should remember him
as if i don't

60

SERPENTINE

pavlov hits me with more bad news every time i answer the phone
so i play and i sing and i just let it ring
all day when i'm at home
a defacto choice of macro
or microcosmic melancholy
but, baby, any way you slice it
i'm thinkin' i could just as soon use the time alone

yes the goons have gone global
and the CEOs are shredding files
and the democrans and the republicrats
are flashing their toothy smiles
uncle tom is posing for a photo op
with the oval office clan
and uncle sam is rigging cockfights
in the promised land
plus that knife you stuck in my back is still there
it pinches a little when i sigh and moan
and these days i'm thinkin' i could just as soon use the time alone

all the wrong people have the power
of suggestion
and the freedom of the press is meaningless
if nobody asks a question
i mean causation by definition
is such a complex compilation of factors
that to even try to say why
is to oversimplify
but that's a far cry, isn't it dear?
from acting like you're the only one there
unrepentantly self-centered and unfair
enter all suckers scrambling for the scoop
exit mr. eye contact
who took his flirt and flew the coop
but whatever

no matter
no fishin' trips
no fishin'
cuz mamma's officially out of commission
and did i mention
in there
somewhere
did i mention
somewhere
in there
that i traded babe ruth?
yes, i traded the only player that was bigger than the game
and i can't even tell you why cuz you'd think i'm insane

and the music industry mafia is pimping girl power
sniping off their sharpshooter singles from their styrofoam towers
and hip hop is tied up in the back room
with a logo stuffed in its mouth
cuz the master's tools will never dismantle the master's house
but then i'm getting away from myself
as i get closer and closer to home
and the difference between you and me baby
is i get fucked up when i'm alone

and i must admit
today my inner pessimist
seems to have got the best of me
we start out sugared up on kool-aid and manifest destiny
and we memorize all the presidents' names
like little trained monkeys
and we're spit into the world
so many spinny-eyed tv junkies
incapable of unravelling the military industrial mystery
preemptively pacified with history book history
and i've been around the world now
and i can see this about america:
the mind control is steep here man
the myopia is deep here man
and behold
those that try to expose the reality
who really try to realize democracy
are shot with rubber bullets and gassed off the streets
while the global power brokers are kept clean and discreet
behind a wall
behind a moat
and that is all
that's all she wrote

and my heart beats an sss o o o sss
cuz folks just couldn't care care care less less less
as long as every day is superbowl sunday
and larger than life women in lingerie
are pouting at us from every bus stop
she loves me   she loves me not
shelovesme shelovesmenot...

"big government should not stand between a man and his money"

"what's good for business is good for the country"

our children still take that lie like communion
the same old line
the confederacy used on the union
conjugate liberty
into libertarian
medicate it
associate it
with deregulation
privatization

we won't even know we're slaves
on a corporate plantation
somebody say hallelujah!
somebody say damnation!
cuz the profit system follows the path of least resistance
and the path of least resistance
is what makes the river crooked
makes it serpentine
capitalism is the devil's wet dream
so just give me my judy garland drugs
and let me get back to work
cuz the empire state building
is the tallest building in new york
and i always got the feeling
you just liked to hear it fall

off your tongue

but i remember my name

in your mouth

and i don't think i was done
hearing it close to my ear
on a whisper's way to a moan
but pavlov hits me with more bad news every time i answer the phone
so i play and i sing and i just let it ring
all day when i'm at home

a defacto choice of macro
or microcosmic melancholy
but baby any way you slice it
i'm thinkin' i could just as soon use
the time alone

thank you audre lorde and utah phillips for the use of your words

TO THE TEETH

the sun is setting on the century
and we are armed to the teeth
we're all working together now
to make our lives mercifully brief
and schoolkids keep trying to teach us
what guns are all about
confuse liberty with weaponry
and watch your kids act it out

and every year now like christmas
some boy gets the milkfed suburban blues
reaches for the available arsenal
and saunters off to make the news
and the women in the middle
are learning what poor women have always known
that the edge is closer than you think
when your men bring the guns home

look at where the profits are
that's how you'll find the source
of the big lie that you and i
both know so well
in the time it takes this cultural
death wish to run its course
they're gonna make a pretty penny
and then they're all going to hell

he said the chickens all come home to roost
yeah, malcolm forecasted this flood
are we really gonna to sleep through another century
while the rich profit off our blood?
true, it may take some doing
to see this undoing through
but in my humble opinion
here's what i suggest we do:

open fire on hollywood
open fire on MTV
open fire on CNN
Fox News and ABC
open fire on the NRA
and all the lies they told us
along the way
open fire on each weapons manufacturer
while he's giving head
to some republican senator

and if i hear one more time
about a fool's right
to his tools of rage
i'm gonna take all my friends
and i'm gonna move to canada
and we're gonna die of old age

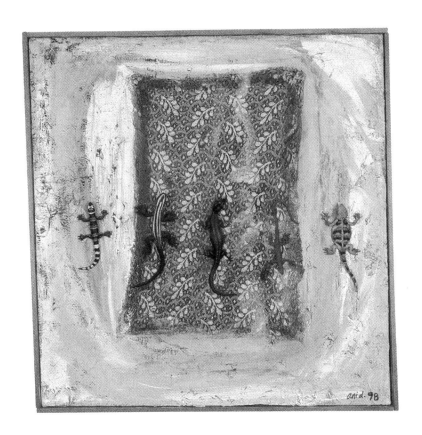

anid. 98

GREY

the sky is grey
the sand is grey
and the ocean is grey
     and i feel right at home
     in this stunning monochrome
     alone in my way

i smoke and i drink
and every time i blink
i have a tiny dream
     but as bad as i am
     i'm proud of the fact
     that i'm worse than i seem

what kind of paradise am i looking for?
i've got everything i want and still i want more
maybe some tiny shiny key will wash up on the shore

you walk through my walls
like a ghost on tv
you penetrate me
     and my little pink heart
     is on its little brown raft
     floating out to sea

and what can i say
but i'm wired this way
and you're wired to me
     and what can i do
     but wallow in you
     unintentionally

what kind of paradise am i looking for?
i've got everything i want and still i want more
maybe some tiny shiny key will wash up on the shore

regretfully
i guess i've only got three
simple things to say:
       why me?
       why this now?
       why this way?

with overtones ringing
and undertows pulling away

       under a sky that is grey
       on sand that is grey
       by an ocean that's grey

what kind of paradise am i looking for?
i've got everything i want and still i want more
maybe some tiny shiny key will wash up on the shore

BODILY

you broke me bodily
the heart ain't the half of it
and i'll never learn to laugh at it
in my good-natured way
in fact i'm laughing less in general
but i learned a lot at my own funeral
and i knew you'd be the death of me
so i guess that's the price i pay

i'm trying to make new memories
in cities where we fell in love
my head just barely above
the darkest waters i've ever known
yeah you had me on that leash
you had me jumpin' through those hoops for you
and still i think i'd stoop for you
stoop for your eyes alone

from that bombshell moon in yet another lovely dress
to the deep mahogany sheen of a roach
i am trying to take an appreciative approach
to life in your wake
i focus on the quiet now
and occasionally i fall asleep somehow
and emptiness has its solace
in that there's nothing left to take

AKIMBO

what dreams cause me
to abandon my pillow each night?

push away each of them in fact
since there always seem to be more than one.

and then wake to aching stiff neck twisted
tits and face smashed against the mattress
legs and arms akimbo

like the high pitched body of a jumper
waiting for her chalk outline
finally at rest.

PLATFORMS

life knocked me off my platforms
so i pulled out my first pair of boots
bought on the street at astor place
before new york was run by suits

and i suited up for the long walk
back to myself
closer to the ground now
with sorrow
and stealth

CAMPING

i love myself when i am camping
because i can walk across a river
on a log
like i am strutting down a runway
i love myself when i am camping
because i can take a dull knife
to a bag of suffering vegetables
and with one flame make a meal
that ain't half bad
i love myself when i am camping
because i can find a way
where there is no trail
because i'm not afraid of spiders
or mud up to my knees
or mice or bees
and because
there are
no mirrors

HYPNOTIZED

so that's how you found me
rain falling around me
lookin' down at a worm
with a long way to go
and the traffic was hissing by
and i was homesick
and i was high

i was surrounded by a language
in which i could say only hello
and thank you very much
but you spoke so i could understand
and i drew a treasure map on your hand

and you were no picnic
you were no prize
but you had just enough pathos
to keep me hypnotized

the map led to an island
in a sea of store-bought dreams
where soulless singers sang
over beats built by machines

and lovely girls were hovering
above my head like gulls
with their long slender necks
and their delicate skulls

and i was no picnic
i was no prize
but i had just enough sweetness
to keep you hypnotized

so that's how you found me
rain falling around me
lookin' down at a worm
with a long way to go

PARAMETERS

thirty-three years go by
and not once do you come home to find a man sitting in your bedroom
that is
a man you don't know
who came a long way to deliver one very specific message:
lock your back door, you idiot.
however invincible you imagine yourself to be
you are wrong.

thirty-three years go by
and you loosen the momentum of teenage nightmares
your breasts hang like a woman's
and you don't jump at shadows anymore
instead you may simply pause to admire
those that move with the grace of trees
dancing past streetlights

and you walk through your house without turning on lamps
sure of the angle from door to table
from table to staircase
sure of the number of steps
seven to the landing
two to turn right
then seven more
sure you will stroll serenely on the moving walkway of memory
across your bedroom
and collapse with a sigh onto your bed
shoes falling
thunk
thunk
onto the floor
and there will be no strange man
suddenly all that time sitting there

sitting there on what must be the prize chair
in your collection of uncomfortable chairs
with a wild look in his eyes
and hands that you cannot see
holding what
you do not know

so sure are you
of the endless drumming rhythm of your isolation
that you are painfully slow to adjust
if only because
yours is not that genre of story

still and again, life cannot muster the stuff of movies
no bullets shattering glass
instead fear sits patiently
fear almost smiles when you finally see him
though you have kept him waiting for thirty-three years
and now he has let himself in
and he has brought you fistfuls of teenage nightmares
though you think you see
in your naivete
that he is empty-handed
and this brings you great relief
at the time

new as you are, really
to the idea that
even after you've long since gotten used to the parameters
they can all change
while you're out one night
having a drink with a friend
some big hand may be turning a big dial
switching channels on your dreams
until you find yourself lost in them
and watching your daily life with the sound off

and of course having cautiously turned down the flame under your eyes
there are more shadows around everything
your vision a dim flashlight that you have to shake all the way to the outhouse
your solitude elevating itself like the spirit of the dead
presiding over your supposed repose
not really sleep at all
just a sleeping position and a series of suspicious sounds
a clanking pipe
a creaking branch
the footfalls of a cat

all of this and maybe
the swish of the soft leather
of your intruder's coat
as you walk him step by step back to the door
having talked him down off the ledge of a very bad idea

soft leather, big feet, almond eyes
the kinds of details the police officer would ask for later
with his clipboard
and his pistol
in your hallway

REPRIEVE

manhattan is an island
like the women who are
surrounded by children in a car
surrounded by cars
or manhattan was a project
that projected the worst of mankind
first one and then the other
has made its mark on my mind

it's sixty years later
near the hypo-center of the a-bomb
i'm in the middle of hiroshima
watching a twisted old eucalyptus tree wave
one of the very few lives that survived and lives on
remembering the day it was suddenly
thousands of degrees in the shade
and what all of nature gave birth to
terror took in a blinding ray
with the kind of pain it would take cancer
so many years just to say

oh to grow up gagged and blindfolded
a man's world in your little girl's head
the voice of the great mother drowned out
in the constant honking
haunting the car crash up ahead
oh to grow up hypnotized
and then try to shake yourself awake
cuz you can sense what has been lost
cuz you can sense what is at stake

yeah, so
it took me a few years to catch on
that those days i catch everyone's eye
correspond with those nights of the month
when the moon gleams like an egg in the sky
and men are using a sense they don't even know they have
just to watch me walk by
and me, i'm supposed to be sensible
leave my animal outside to cry
but when all of nature conspires
to make me her glorious whore
it's cuz in my body i hold the secret recipe
of precisely what life is for
and the patriarchy that looks to shame me for it
is the same one making war
and i've said too much already
but i'll tell you something more

to split yourself in two
is just the most radical thing you can do
so girl if that shit ain't up to you
then you simply are not free
cuz from the sunlight on my hair
to which eggs i grow to term
to the expression that i wear
all i really own is me
yes to split yourself in two
is just the most radical thing you can do
goddess forbid that little atom
should grow so jealous of eve

and in the face of the great farce
of the nuclear age
feminism ain't about equality
it's about reprieve

GRAND CANYON

i love my country
by which i mean i am indebted joyfully
to all the people throughout its history
who have fought the government to make right
where so many cunning sons and daughters
our foremothers and forefathers
came singing through slaughter
came through hell and high water
so that we could stand here
and behold breathlessly the sight
how a raging river of tears
cut a grand canyon of light

yes i've been a lot of places
flown through vast empty spaces
with stewardesses whose hands
look much older than their faces
and i've tossed so many napkins
into that big hole in the sky
bin at the bottom of the atlantic
seething in a two-ply
looking up through all that water
and the fishes swimming by
and i don't always feel lucky
but i'm smart enough to try
cuz humility has buoyancy
and above us only sky

so i lean in
breathe deeper that brutal burning smell
that surrounds the smoldering wreckage
that i've come to love so well
yes, color me stunned and dazzled
by all the red white and blue flashing lights
in the american intersection
where black crashed head on with white
comes a melody
comes a rhythm
a particular resonance
that is us and only us
comes a screaming ambulance
and a hand that you can trust
laid steady on your chest
working for the better good
(which is good at its best)
and too, bearing witness
like a woman bears a child

with all her might

born of the greatest pain
into a grand canyon of light

i mean no song has gone unsung here
and this joint is strung crazy tight
and people here bin raising up their voices
since it just ain't bin right
with all the righteous rage
and all the bitter spite
that will accompany us out
of this long night
that will grab us by the hand
when we are ready to take flight
seatback and traytable in the upright and locked position
shocked to tears by each new vision

of all that my ancestors have done
like say
the women who gave their lives
so that i could have one
people, we are standing at ground zero of the feminist revolution!
yeah it was an inside job, stoic and sly
one we're supposed to forget and downplay and deny
but i think the time is nothing
if not nigh
to let the truth out
coolest f-word ever deserves a fucking shout!
i mean why don't all decent men and women call themselves feminists?
if only out of respect
for those who fought for this
i mean look around

we have this.

yes
i love my country
by which i mean
i am indebted joyfully
to all the people throughout its history
who have fought the government to make right
where so many cunning sons and daughters
our foremothers and forefathers
came singing through slaughter
came through hell and high water
so that we could stand here
and behold breathlessly the sight
how a raging river of tears
is cutting a grand canyon of light

THE INTERVIEW

how can one speak on
the role of politics in art
when art is
activism?

and anyway
both are just a lifelong light
shining through a swinging prism.

ANI AND SEKOU SUNDIATA
IN CONVERSATION

*In 1990 at the age of eighteen, Ani DiFranco rewrote the rules
of the record industry when she created her own label Righteous Babe
Records as an alternative to beckoning corporate offices. Since then,
RBR has released nineteen full-length DiFranco albums to
critical acclaim, and is now home to over a dozen cutting-edge new
artists. DiFranco was named one of the top twenty-five most
influential artists of the past twenty-five years by* CMJ New Music
*(alongside Nirvana and U2) and one of the top twenty-one feminists
of the twenty-first century by* Ms. Magazine. *She lives in Buffalo,
New York, and New Orleans, Louisiana.*

*Harlem-born Sekou Sundiata is one of America's most notable
spoken-word poets and innovators of contemporary poetry, known
for his fusing of various black cultural traditions and his unique
interbreeding of music and poetry. A longtime teacher of literature
at The New School, he has inspired many poets and artists, most
notably, Ani DiFranco. He lives in New York City.*

The poem "Literal" is a gem, something that poetry anthologies and poetry teachers would love. I talk to my students a lot about how poetry asks us to try seeing double—that is, beyond literal. To see the molecular world (our bodies, the daily news, the earth, etc.) and to also see the powers that animate that world. I think I've spent my whole life seeing double—being fixed, mystified, and mesmerized by those powers. Somebody said: anything can make us look, but art can make us see. Do you think this kind of spooky action at a distance brought you to poetry in the first place? Or was it something else?

Ani   Spooky action at a distance. Gotta love Einstein! Back when I was a student in your classes, you taught me that poetry is not just writing in long skinny columns, but more a way of seeing, and I think I inherently understood you because I share your double vision. I think, to an extent, that everyone does—until we have it socialized out of us. I am holding my new little four-month-old baby in my left arm while I write with my right, and she is a constant reminder to me of how intuitive and capable of multidimensional awareness the human animal is by nature. She does nothing but use the force all day long, completely unconfused or distracted by linguistically structured thought. She seems to really sense all the energy and intention around her. Socialization—the process by which we are drawn into society—can create a cloud between us and our nature, and between us and our awareness of the powers that animate and connect things. It's funny to me that society uses language to divert our attention away from being present, because it is also with language that the poet pierces that cloud and shines light once again on awareness. To engage with poetry, we must free our minds of the constrictions of linear thought, and exercise the fluidity of our pre-language awakeness and creativity. I love poetry's ability to make us feel what is beyond knowing, and yes, I think that's what drew me to it.

Sekou   I see a theme that comes up again and again. Desire and personal love is somehow linked to a larger love: community, country, etc. I am thinking of "Subdivision," where you address your city. And in "Coming Up":

> i was trying to love someone again
> i was caught caring
> bearing weight
> but i love this city
> this state
> this country

This comes across to me as a kind of Old Left sensibility. I mean that in a good way. Those old radicals wanted to transform society, for sure, but they also had a deep love for the country. I connect this also to the strain of the folk music tradition that comes out of that. Does this make sense?

Ani	Absolutely! I am a product of the Old Left, or a disciple, if you will. Old lefties have been my promoters, employers, teachers, and comrades since I busted onto the folk circuit as a teenager. Much of my formative years were spent at folk festivals, community halls, coffeehouses, and political demonstrations where I learned about America's radical continuum from those who were still living it. I was also traveling around America itself, growing an appreciation for all of its fascinating cultures and jaw-dropping landscapes. I was falling for the endless allure of America, and I had people like Utah Phillips and Mark Twain before him giving me the language to define my newfound patriotism. "The country is the real thing," said Twain, "the substantial thing, the eternal thing, it is the thing to watch over, and care for, and to be loyal to; institutions are extraneous, they are its mere clothing and clothing can wear out..."

I learned to distinguish between America and the government of America, and realized that loving one can often mean being willing to take action against the other. When you know your own history—not the history of the ruling class but the people's history—it is cause for great pride and loyalty! When I look at the vilification of socialism and how the Old Left was crushed in America, it looks a lot like the modern vilification of feminism, which is to say, the work of another calculated marketing campaign. As threatened as power is by the recognition of class structure (let alone patriarchy!), it is petrified of the ideal of having the owning class be responsible to the working class. Meanwhile, the Old Left was often beautifully united across race and sex lines, and in constant cross-pollination with dynamic artistic movements. The repeated covert persecution of radicals by the American government is especially saddening to me because I believe that what socialism has been missing in practice around the world is exactly what America can bring to it: a respect for the purely aesthetic side of human nature and freedom of expression. As the women factory workers in the Ludlow Textile strike proclaimed: we need bread, yes, but we need roses too! We need to do more than survive, we need the time and the opportunity to be self-realized people. Bread and roses. The poetry of the Old Left sings in my ears.

Sekou	*In "Fuel" I recognize you as the poet taking up the prophetic voice by seeing double. These poems know that we are on the edge, and they tilt towards a response to that precarious position. The most useful response is personal freedom and autonomy. In that sense, these poems are freedom songs. To me, they can be seen as a kind of democratic enterprise.*

I get the sense that while you acknowledge the aloneness of being human you also recognize that aloneness is variable. Sometimes it's a solitude that spells isolation and loneliness, other times it is a true space of companionship with one's self and spirit. This is another way for me to say that the "I" in these poems understands the burden and the sanctity of the individual self and, at the same time, the need for that self to connect to something larger: art, community, etc. This to me is a democratic notion: the space for the individual to be different and the space to belong.

Ani   I will cop to being a lover of democracy! Democracy without participation is meaningless, as we can see evidenced in the corporate states of America, but democracy-in-action is, I believe, one of the most highly evolved political solutions to the ongoing crisis in which we are made to live. To be awake to the fact of oppression and exploitation all around us is to be faced with a choice: respond and make yourself accountable, or accept and make yourself as comfortable as possible, given the circumstances. But what I learned from all those old lefties along the way is, democracy works. Everything that we collectively hold great about America was fought for and won by activists and artists. From the organizers of the Boston Tea Party, to the abolitionists and the suffragettes, to the union organizers who brought you the weekend, from the American Indian movement, to the Black Panthers, to ACT-UP, America has been transformed by people of revolutionary thought and spirit. As my friend Utah would say, freedom is something we are born with, like our eyes and our ears. Then we wait for someone to come along and try to take it away. The degree to which we resist is the degree to which we are free. When I look at things like peace and justice in this world, naturally, it is my womanhood that looks. And I see patriarchy at the root of social injustice and war. Patriarchy, an undisputed fact of human society, is inherently imbalanced, and nature favors balance. I believe the shift in consciousness that is a prerequisite to peace is the very one that will occur through the total empowerment and participation of women in society. When we will finally incorporate ideas like personal freedom and autonomy, with the understanding that no one exists except in relationship to others. This interplay between masculine and feminine wisdom, in the world around me and within myself, is at the core of my writer's voice, my life experience, and my political ideals.

Sekou   *One of the other sets of themes I see in these poems relate to this defiance, resistance, and commitment to personal autonomy. From "32 Flavors":*

> *i'm beyond your peripheral vision*
> *so you might wanna turn your head*
> *cuz some day you are going to get hungry*
> *and eat most of the words you just said*

At the same time, your poems and songs never let me forget that all that defiance and resistance is in the service of a new and improved way of living in the world, of feeling and thinking about the world. These things come together in my mind as the Righteous Babe expression, meaning the critique is not gratuitous or disconnected from the body and the spirit. Any thoughts?

93

Ani   I think the basis of my social defiance is the very thing that distinguishes
me from the power structure: my gender. The sport of life as a 5' 2" female
in a man's world (with the upped ante of being emancipated at the age of fifteen)
gives me a particular insight into certain power dynamics between people. And
being a teenage girl living alone, my process of self-empowerment was
not at all theoretical but something of a full-time occupation, so I've always
written a lot about it. Of course, I didn't realize setting out how useful that
expression could be to others, especially other young women. The name
"righteous babe" came out of an ongoing joke between me and my best friend
in high school. We thought the constant cat-calling of men funny, as we moved
through the streets as young women. "Hey baby! Yo baby! Wanna ride with me?
What's your name, babe?" So we appropriated the term "babe," and started calling
it to each other. It was a wholly intuitive form of self-empowerment, similar
to the modern young black man calling his pals his "niggas." The "righteous" part
came shortly thereafter as a way, I think, of expressing that a young woman can
be alive and sexual, but also self-possessed and strong. The artificial dichotomy
between the stereotypes of the humorless, un-sexy feminist and the boy-toy
girlie girl struck me as bullshit. I guess it is fair to say that the recognition of
the righteous babe in me was my invocation into a world of political resistance
based in body, breath, and consciousness.

Sekou   *I have always been struck by your sharp wit and your humor. "My IQ" is a good example:*

                 they asked me
                 which one is different and does not belong?
                 they taught me different
                 is wrong

*This, to me, is not about saying something clever. It is a kind of blue truth that the best
comedians understood: Lenny Bruce, Richard Pryor. You obviously find great joy
in the world, but you also find these humorous, sometimes biting insights when you look
at the world. Where does that come from, how does it work its way into your poems?
I've seen you perform enough times to know that you also have great timing in terms
of how and when you deliver those lines. I would call it a comedian's or storyteller's timing.
Do you relate to this line of thinking about your poetry?*

Ani   Funny you should mention Lenny Bruce. He's been hero of mine since
        I was eighteen. And later Richard Pryor, and also Bill Hicks. I have always loved
        and adored, learned from and related to, these comedians. Comedians who,
        as you say, are storytellers who use humor to get people to tilt their heads back
        and open their throats up wide with laughter so that then they can make them
        swallow something really big. These are artists who have really fulfilled the fabled
        role of poet in modern society: delivering truth in such potent doses, and
        providing social commentary so vital, that each of them suffered personally in
        exchange. I have taken a lot from them in terms of my own performance for sure.
        I have been hugely inspired by their sheer bravery. Watching people like Bruce
        and Pryor walk onto a stage and say the unspeakable inspired me immeasurably
        towards being candid in my own writing and performance. To me they represent
        the willingness to sacrifice comfort and popularity for the sake of something bigger.

Sekou   *You have such a distinctive approach and voice as a performer. I wonder if you think that
        some poems are better suited to performance than to publication? If so, how do you decide?*

Ani   The difference between the spoken word and the written word has long intrigued
        me, and the journey that this body of work took—from the page to the stage and
        back again—was long and mysterious. It is hard for me to grasp how my poems
        read on paper because when I try to read them my spoken voice echoes loudly
        in my ears. I've performed them so many times that to me they read like the
        transcript of a testimony.

        "Transcript" might have been a good name for this book, but it wouldn't express
        nearly as well the overlap of poem and song, while not ruling out the notion that
        all of these works could simply be verses in the one long rambling folk song of me.

        For years, making a book has been suggested to me, but I was unready to stay
        still long enough to realize the idea. At home now, taking a crash course in
        mothering, it finally seemed like the right time. Making this book excited my
        intuition, challenged my understanding of my own voice, and felt a bit like
        trying to take photographs of clouds. These are some hard-traveling poems.
        Whether or not they were initially built for performance or publication, I am
        pleased that they have finally found a place to rest together.

ani

photo by Danny Clinch